THE
WORKBOOK
ON
DOWNSIZING

When Monika Lowry and her husband, Robert Miller, reflect on the life they've built together, they can't help but smile. Self-professed soul mates, it was a long and winding road to arrive here and, in their words, fulfill their destiny. Life threatening illnesses, cross-continent voyages, tireless hard work, Monika and Robert have faced enough adversity for two lifetimes and made some extremely difficult choices along the way. Still, both will tell you they consider themselves all the wiser – and stronger – for it.

Having experienced more struggle than she'd care to recall before her seventh birthday, Monika still manages to be one of the most animated, positive individuals you'll ever encounter. She is also a successful business woman, passionate world traveller, and voracious reader with a zest for life that is nothing less than infectious. "I believe each day you have a choice to be happy and I willingly make that choice" she says.

Robert admires and shares his wife's outlook. After a health scare in 1991, he vowed to make the most of every day and never take anything for granted. A prolific and articulate writer, speaker and creative thinker, Robert has successfully blended his 40 years of face-to-face corporate and Real Estate client conversations with Monika's insights and wisdom to create "The Book on Downsizing".

THE
WORKBOOK
ON
DOWNSIZING

7 Steps to Rightsize the Rest of Your Life

Robert Miller
& Monika Lowry

ISBN 13: 978-0-9881611-3-9

Visit www.TheBookonDownsizing.com for FREE Resources and to learn more.

FOREWORD

What if you could turn back time and change the life you have lived till now! While this may not be possible, we do have the opportunity to change our future and create the lifestyle we want in our "Next Chapter" of life. How? Simply, by planning.

The Book on Downsizing is a guided tour to developing your personalized *Downsizing Plan* by answering the "Who, *What, When, Why, How, and Where*" for that incredible *journey* ahead. *"Designing the Next Chapter of your life"* will be simpler and more enjoyable by utilizing this *Downsizing Planning* process with all of the insights, tools and exercises, including:

A. How Downsizing is a process not an event

B. Why Downsizing encompasses your lifestyle choices, as well as, your home

C. When Downsizing is about "moving on" versus "hanging on"

D. How Downsizing starts with simple planning

E. Who Downsizing is a team sport with

F. How Downsizing can be the most exciting journey of your life

G. Why Downsizing requires your personal action now

Most Baby Boomers or "Zoomers" have been disciplined and careful to set aside a nest egg to fund the lifestyle they envisioned for their post-working years. Others, who have enjoyed the good life, arrive rather unprepared. In either case, many of us are healthy enough to be retired for more years than we actually worked so it is crucial that we "plan ahead".

Prepared or not, many of us have already arrived and "The Book on Downsizing" provides a candid, uplifting perspective to help prepare us for *the best chapter of our life,* those unspent days that lie ahead! While emptying our closets or buying that smaller home may be one of the end results, there's lots of pre-work before we get there and this book walks you through the 7 steps that facilitate the right conclusions for you and your partner.

Successful Baby Boomers themselves, Robert Miller and Monika Lowry bring 5 decades of combined experience helping their clients *"choose the home they'll love to live in"*. Drawing on more than 10,000 hours of personal face-to-face interviews with home buyers and sellers, they bring a wealth of experience and a candid, heartfelt perspective.

As both business and life partners, Monika and Robert are early adopters who have been there and "walked the walk" themselves. So whether you find yourself looking at *Downsizing, Rightsizing, or Shifting Gears in mid stream*, this book offers wonderful insights and the tools that will help you and your partner *"design the Next Chapter"* of your life, together........ and live it with passion and purpose.

Raymond Aaron,

New York Times bestselling author of *Chicken Soup for the Canadian Soul, Chicken Soup for the Parent's Soul*, and *Double Your Income Doing What You Love*

INTRODUCTION

As explained in *The Book on Downsizing*, there are three related concepts that characterize the kinds of changes that couples (or individuals) often make as they enter their later lives:

Downsizing is a process of re-engineering your life, where you seek to analyse, simplify, and determine what really matters to you and your partner in your "Next Chapter." Together, you define your individual and shared goals, expectations, and priorities.

Rightsizing is a process in which you seek to reclaim the lifestyle you've put on hold... until now! For some, it's realizing their dream of that large country home, a year-round home at the lake, or perhaps the equestrian farm with stables and acres of fenced paddocks. It's a time to consider desires that have been deferred. If this describes you, then you may be a rightsizer.

Shifting Gears is typically a pre-retirement process in which, as it sounds, you make changes in your activities or way of doing things. It may be the decision to buy a business, change careers, or step away from a high-profile political or corporate role to devote more time to your family or health. Shifting gears may be a proactive choice or a response to changes in your personal health, career or business.

"DOWNSIZING MEANS DIFFERENT THINGS TO DIFFERENT PEOPLE..."

"RIGHTSIZING IS THE FULFILLMENT OF THOSE LIFESTYLE DREAMS YOU PUT ON HOLD TO FOCUS ON YOUR CAREER AND FAMILY"

"SHIFTING GEARS IS STEPPING OUT OF OUR TRADITIONAL COMFORT ZONE TO DESIGN THE REST OF OUR LIFE, OUR WAY!"

Where To Start?

For many of us, celebrating the "Big Five-O" brought with it the realization that our lives were changing. For some, it saw the dawning of opportunities that we had waited and worked for throughout our careers. For others, it brought the fear that time was running out and that the financial security we had hoped for and invested in had been derailed by circumstances beyond our control.

While the experience may have been very different for each of us, the reality is that time advances at the same rate for everyone and we all need to plan for our Next Chapter. To do that, we need to answer key questions that will shape the future that we share with our partner. These are:

A. What Does Downsizing Mean to Me?

B. When Should I Downsize?

C. Why Is Downsizing Important to Me?

D. Who Am I Downsizing With?

E. How Much Can I Afford in the Next Chapter?

F. Where Do I Want to Downsize?

What is the purpose of this Personal Downsizing Profile?

The Book on Downsizing helps you understand HOW to develop your Next Chapter Plan. This workbook helps you transform ***HOW into NOW!*** We created *The Book on Downsizing* at the urging of our many clients after more than 10,000 hours of face-to-face conversations with couples making the myriad decisions associated with buying and selling their home. This book is designed to help you take action—that is, to turn ***HOW into NOW!***

> "THE BOOK ON DOWNSIZING IS A SIMPLE STEP-BY-STEP GUIDE TO DESIGNING THE REST OF YOUR LIFE"

As with any decision-making process, having the relevant information readily available is invaluable in helping you work wisely and efficiently. Your responses to the assessments in this workbook can serve as an excellent resource in facilitating a "focused conversation between you and your partner."

It's exciting to discover those areas where you are in agreement, and helpful to see where you have diverging perspectives. Through ongoing dialogue, couples can discern what is most important to each of them and make choices that will allow them to design the Next Chapter of the life they want to live together.

> "MANY OF US WILL PUT OFF REALIZING OUR UNFULFILLED LIFE DREAMS UNTIL WE FIND THE TIME, BUT WILL IT BE TOO LATE?"

Typically, couples also rediscover many unfulfilled wishes, hopes, and dreams that were pushed aside during their frenetic working years. These should be included in your "Bucket List," another resource in this workbook that will assist you in designing the rest of your life.

We encourage you and your spouse or life partner to each complete a profile, so that you will be able to compare your responses and get the most out of the several assessment resources available to you.

MY DOWNSIZING PROFILE - A PERSONAL PLANNING RESOURCE

A. Name _____

B. Spouse or Partner's name _____

C. As defined in the Introduction to *The Book on Downsizing*, my partner and I believe that in our Next Chapter we want to:

    1. Downsize ☐

    2. Rightsize ☐

    3. Shift Gears ☐

D. In what decade were you born? 30s ☐ 40s ☐ 50s ☐ 60s ☐ 70s ☐ 80s ☐

E. Where were you born? (country & state or province) _____ / _____

F. Typically, my best friends are:

    1. Older than I am ☐

    2. About the same age as I am ☐

    3. Younger than I am ☐

G. Did you graduate from high school? ☐ Yes ☐ No

H. Did you attend college or university? ☐ Yes ☐ No

    1. If so, how many years did you attend? _____

    2. What was your major and minor in university or college? _____

    3. Did you complete a postgraduate degree? ☐ Yes ☐ No

    4. Did you enjoy your postsecondary school years? ☐ Yes ☐ No

    5. If you could return to school, would you like to? ☐ Yes ☐ No

    6. If so, what would you study this time? _____

I. What is your favorite pastime (sport, hobby, or activity)? _____

J. What type of activities do you prefer?

    1. Participating in a group ☐

    2. Individual activities ☐

K. Do you see yourself as a competitive person? ☐ Yes ☐ No

L. If you could turn back time, would you want to be 30 again? ☐ Yes ☐ No

    1. Why or why not? _____

You are now ready to begin developing your Downsizing Plan.

The following resources will assist you in making the choices that are right for you and help you create your personalized Downsizing Plan based on your Next Chapter lifestyle goals and expectations.

HAVE FUN - PLANNING AND ANTICIPATION ARE AN IMPORTANT PART OF THE JOURNEY!

1

MY DOWNSIZING QUESTIONS ANSWERED:
WHAT DOES DOWNSIZING MEAN TO ME?

I. What is your vision of the rest of your life (as it relates to working, playing, and giving back)

A. Do you have a vision for the rest of your life? ☐ Yes ☐ No

1. If yes, what is it? _____

_____

_____

_____

B. Does your spouse/partner have a vision for the rest of their life? ☐ Yes ☐ No

1. If yes, what do you understand it to be? _____

_____

_____

_____

C. What brings the most meaning and enjoyment in your daily life (a thing, person, or activity)?

_____

_____

D. How would you like to be remembered? _____

1. What could you do today to make that 1 reality? _____

_____

_____

_____

NOTES

E Make a list of the 5 organizations where you can volunteer and make a difference:

1. _____

2. _____

3. _____

4. _____

5. _____

F. What person in your past was your greatest inspiration? _____

1. What are three things you can do in your own life to follow their example?

a. _____

b. _____

c. _____

G. Do you prefer participating in group activities or individual pursuits? _____

H. What individual skills or talents would you like to explore and utilize in the Next Chapter of your lives to maintain passion and purpose?

1. _____

2. _____

3. _____

4. _____

5. _____

I. What was your primary career, job or business during your working years? _____

_____

J. How many years did you work in this field? _____

NOTES

K. Did you enjoy your work? _____

    1. Have you retired?

        a. Yes _____ When? _____

        b. No _____ Do you plan to retire? _____ When (approx. date) _____

        c. Would you like to continue working (if given the choice)? _____

        d. Do you feel you will _need_ to continue working beyond age 65? ☐ Yes ☐ No

            i. If yes, why?

                • I need to continue earning _____

                • I enjoy working and it keeps me young _____

                • I feel healthier when I work _____

L. If you had the choice to do it again, what career would you have chosen?

_____

_____

Why?

_____

_____

II. If you could change or improve something in your life, what would it be?

A. Finances _____

    1. Are your financial resources sufficient for your Next Chapter? ☐ Yes ☐ No

        a. If no, what is your plan to address this?

            i. _____

            ii. _____

            iii. _____

            iv. _____

NOTES

B. Relationships _____

    1. Relationships, like finances, require both deposits and withdrawals along the way. Do you have a good relationship with your partner or spouse? ☐ Yes ☐ No

        a. If no, what is your plan to rebuild it?

           i. _____

           ii. _____

           iii. _____

    2. Investing our time and skills with passion and purpose keeps us young and alive. How are you investing your time today that keeps you vibrant and feeling alive?

        a. _____

        b. _____

        c. _____

    3. Are you a positive person whose social skills and outlook attract others? ☐ Yes ☐ No

        a. If yes, what makes you happy and upbeat?

           i. _____

           ii. _____

           iii. _____

    4. If no, what steps are you willing to take to rediscover yourself and your life?

        a. _____

        b. _____

        c. _____

Notes

2

My Downsizing Questions Answered:

When Should I Downsize?

I. Understanding the driving forces that make this the right time

A. Health

1. Do you have chronic ailments that could affect your enjoyment of the Next Chapter you envision? ☐ Yes ☐ No

2. Are you experiencing progressive midlife ailments such as declining energy, increasing stiffness and lack of mobility? ☐ Yes ☐ No

3. Are you concerned that your health is beginning to impact your ability to enjoy travelling? ☐ Yes ☐ No

4. Will you need to renovate or make a move to accommodate the declining mobility of you or your partner? ☐ Yes ☐ No

B. Career, Job and Business

1. Is retiring something you are looking forward to? ☐ Yes ☐ No

2. Are you at risk of being displaced at work? ☐ Yes ☐ No

3. Do you own your own business? ☐ Yes ☐ No

   a. If yes, do you have a succession plan? ☐ Yes ☐ No

   b. If no, what is your exit strategy? _____

C. Personal Finances

1. Will your financial plan allow you to retire today? ☐ Yes ☐ No

   If no, when will you be able to retire? _____

2. Will you need to continue working in retirement? ☐ Yes ☐ No

   If yes, will your health and skills make it viable? ☐ Yes ☐ No

3. Are today's market returns deferring your retirement date? ☐ Yes ☐ No

   a. Other Investments

      i. Do you have real estate or other investments ☐ Yes ☐ No

         • Would these investments allow you to retire now? ☐ Yes ☐ No

NOTES

3

MY DOWNSIZING QUESTIONS ANSWERED:

WHY IS DOWNSIZING IMPORTANT TO ME?

I. **Are you excited about the Next Chapter opportunities that lie ahead?**
□ Yes   □ No

  A. If no, what is missing that would inspire you or give you purpose?

    i. _____

    ii. _____

    iii. _____

II. **Downsizing is like a "cleanse" that allows you to do some "spring cleaning" by redefining yourself and determining what really matters. What work do you need to do regarding:**

  A. Your home?

    i. _____

    ii. _____

    iii. _____

  B. Your relationship with your partner?

    i. _____

    ii. _____

    iii. _____

NOTES

C. Your business environment?

    i. _____

    ii. _____

    iii. _____

III. Downsizing causes you to stop, assess where you are, and develop your Next Chapter Plan:

A. What are your three proudest achievements in life?

    i. _____

    ii. _____

    iii. _____

B. What three failures have you learned the most from?

    i. _____

    ii. _____

    iii. _____

C. How would you rate your health and well-being? _____ (Rate 1- 5 with 5 being highest)

D. Have you met your Next Chapter financial target? ☐ Yes ☐ No

    i. If no, do you have a plan to address this? ☐ Yes ☐ No

        a. If yes, what is it?

        _____

        _____

        _____

NOTES

E. Do you have balance between the stress of being too active and the boredom of having too little to do?
☐ Yes   ☐ No

   i. If no, how could you address this in a positive way?

      a. _____

      b. _____

      c. _____

F. Does the trilogy of the "*Would Haves, Could Haves, Should Haves*" in your life still haunt you?
☐ Yes   ☐ No

   i. If yes, what steps would allow you to move on?

      a. _____

      b. _____

      c. _____

NOTES

4

MY DOWNSIZING QUESTIONS ANSWERED:
WHO AM I DOWNSIZING WITH?

I. Do you have a life partner?

A. ☐ Yes ☐ No

B. If yes:

    i.   Married ☐ How Many Years Together _____

    ii. Partners ☐ How Many Years Together _____

II. Are you and your partner/spouse looking forward to the Next Chapter together?

A. Yes: (check all that apply)

    i.   We are very happy together ☐

    ii. We enjoy spending time together ☐

    iii. We enjoy travelling together ☐

    iv. We enjoy shared pursuits ☐

    v.   We enjoy parallel pursuits ☐

    vi. We share the same friends ☐

    vii. Other: _____

NOTES

B. No: (check all that apply)

    i.   We are friends, but not in love anymore ☐

    ii. We love each other, but "the bloom is off the rose" ☐

    iii. We are carrying too much "personal baggage" ☐

    iv. I believe a shared external focus could help us ☐

    v. I do not believe our relationship is salvageable ☐

    vi. I am willing to work at it, but my partner is not ☐

III. Do you and your partner / spouse share a vision for the rest of your lives (i.e., have agreed-upon goals)?

A. Yes, our shared vision is to:

_____

_____

_____

B. No:

    i.   My partner and I cannot agree on what we want for the future ☐ Yes   ☐ No

    ii. My partner and I are anxious about our future together due to:

        a. Health issues ☐

            i.   My health ☐

            ii. My partner's health ☐

        b. Financial pressures ☐

            i.   Too much debt ☐

            ii. Lack of retirement savings ☐

        c. Support commitments to others:

            i.   Children ☐

            ii. Adult children ☐

            iii. Parents ☐

NOTES

      iv. A disabled dependent ☐

         1. In our home ☐

         2. Outside our home ☐

   d. Relationship challenges ☐

   e. Lack of shared interests ☐

   6. Accumulated emotional baggage ☐

   7. Other: _____

IV. Is spending more time with your partner important to you? ☐ Yes ☐ No

A. If yes:

   i. How do you reinvest in keeping your relationship alive?

     1. Movie nights ☐

     2. Weekly date nights ☐

     3. Dinner at home most nights ☐

     4. Weekend outings ☐

     5. Day trips ☐

     6. Shared hobbies (e.g., golf, tennis, fitness, running) ☐

     7. Annual vacation (1-3 weeks) ☐

     8. Extended travel (4–24 weeks) ☐

     9. Other:

       i. _____

       ii. _____

       iii. _____

NOTES

V. Is pursuing a venture together a shared dream? ☐ Yes ☐ No

    A. If yes, my partner and I have dreamed of starting a business together ☐

        i. Bed & Breakfast ☐

        ii. Restaurant or catering business ☐

        iii. Trendy boutique ☐

        iv. Franchise ☐

        v. Studio ☐

        vi. Other:

            a. _____

            b. _____

            c. _____

VI. We have dreamed of buying a boat and sailing part of each year ☐ Yes ☐ No

    A. Caribbean ☐

    B. Mediterranean ☐

    C. Great Lakes ☐

    D. Other:

        i. _____

        ii. _____

        iii. _____

NOTES

VII. Our dream is a large motor home and extensive travelling ☐ Yes ☐ No

    A. We love the adventure of seeing new places ☐

    B. We love the social aspect – always meeting new people ☐

    C. We love the freedom of being away and unreachable ☐

    D. We love the time it gives us to be alone, together ☐

    E. Other:

        i. _____

        ii. _____

        iii. _____

VIII. Is your dream to return to school? ☐ Yes ☐ No   Then, If Yes:

    A. I graduated from high school, but want a college degree ☐

    B. I went to college or university and want to upgrade ☐

    C. I just love learning and don't care about credits ☐

    D. I want to share this study experience with my partner ☐

    E. If I returned to school, I would study:

        i. _____

        ii. _____

        iii. _____

NOTES

IX. All my life I have wanted to pursue my passion of:

A. Art ☐

B. Music ☐

C. Woodworking ☐

D. Writing ☐

E. Building my nostalgia car ☐

F. Riding a Harley ☐

G. Travelling endlessly ☐

H. I want to share this passion with my partner ☐

    i. Other passions:

        i. _____

        ii. _____

        iii. _____

X. My partner and I enjoy parallel pursuits (doing different things at same time)

A. My favorite pursuits are:

    i. _____

    ii. _____

    iii. _____

B. My partner's favorite pursuits are:

    i. _____

    ii. _____

    iii. _____

NOTES

5

MY DOWNSIZING AFFORDABILITY PROFILE
HOW MUCH CAN I AFFORD IN THE "NEXT CHAPTER"?

Part A

How Much Can I Afford in the "Next Chapter"?

PLEASE NOTE!

Like other sections of this assessment, the information will help to ensure that you and your partner are "on the same page," in this case with regard to your current financial position and direction.

This can assist in assessing your current position, as well as evaluating your projected financial resources relative to your "Next Chapter" lifestyle and Bucket List expectations.

TO LIVE THE "NEXT CHAPTER" LIFESTYLE YOU HAVE DREAMED OF, IT'S IMPORTANT TO PULL TOGETHER A SUMMARY OF ALL OUR FINANCIAL RESOURCES.

I. Budgeting for Our "Next Chapter" Home:

A. Target purchase price of our "Next Chapter" home = $ _____

B. Maximum price we are willing to spend for a perfect "10" = $ _____

C. Owning an impressive home with these features is high on our "Bucket List."   ☐ Yes   ☐ No

D. Approximate number of years we expect to live in this home is _____

E. We also anticipate purchasing a seasonal home.   ☐ Yes   ☐ No

　　1. If Yes, the target purchase price of our seasonal home = $ _____

NOTES

II. Income Earning Capacity:

A. I am currently working:

    1. Full-time employee? ☐ Yes   ☐ No

    2. My estimated monthly income (before taxes) $ _____

    3. My employer offers a company pension plan. ☐ Yes   ☐ No

        a. I choose to participate ☐

        b. I choose not to participate ☐

    4. Part-time employee   ☐ Yes   ☐ No

        a. My estimated monthly income (before taxes) $ _____

    5. On Contract: ☐ Yes   ☐ No

        a. My estimated monthly income (before taxes) $ _____

B. Job Security:

    1. I am concerned that my position may go away (declared surplus):

        a. I believe I will receive a reasonable severance ☐

        b. I believe any severance pay will be inadequate to support me ☐

    2. I am concerned that I may be let go:

        a. My company or department is not doing well ☐

        b. I am struggling in my job and not doing well ☐

        c. Circumstances outside my control (politics, health) ☐

C. I am not currently working:

    1. I am currently retired ☐ Retirement Date: _____/_____

    2. I am actively looking for another job ☐

    3. I am concerned about finding another job in my field ☐

    4. I currently receive support (Severance, Disability, Unemployment Insurance) ☐

        a. This is sufficient to support my needs ☐

        b. This is insufficient and I am eroding my savings & equity ☐

NOTES

III. Current Outstanding Debt:

   A.   How many mortgages do you currently have secured by properties? _____

      1.   Estimated value of my home $ _____

      2.   Estimated value of other properties I own $ _____

      3.   Approximate current mortgage balance (on all properties) $ _____

      4.   Outstanding loans (secured by my properties) _____

         i.   Bank loans: approx. balance outstanding = $ _____

         ii.   Car or truck loans (other than with your bank): approx balance= $ _____

         iii.   Loans for other vehicles (boat, motor home, ATV, motorcycle) = $ _____

   B. I currently have a Line of Credit (LOC) ☐ Yes   ☐ No

      1. If Yes:

         i.   My LOC is secured against the equity in my house: ☐ Yes   ☐ No

         ii.   I have an Unsecured Line of Credit: ☐ Yes   ☐ No

         iii.   My outstanding Line(s) Of Credit balance is approx. $ _____ **

            (** If there is more than one, please show total of all LOCs)

   C. Credit cards & charge cards:

      1. How many credit cards (Visa, MasterCard, Amex) do you use? _____

      2. How many other charge cards (e.g., Shell, Walmart, Sears) do you use? _____

         i.   What is the estimated total outstanding balance owed on all of these? $ _____

IV. Savings & Investment:

   A. I have a savings account ☐ Yes   ☐ No

      1. If yes: My savings account balance is approx. $ _____

   B. My company offers a pension plan for employees. ☐ Yes   ☐ No

      1. I am currently working and contributing to this plan. ☐ Yes   ☐ No

NOTES

2. Upon retirement, I have been advised that I can expect to earn approx. $ _____
   per month

   i. Please check whether 1 or 2 (below) applies to your monthly pension plan earnings received after retirement:

      a. Guaranteed for as long as I live (with no cap) ☐ Yes ☐ No

      b. No guarantee (i.e., ongoing income available is based on performance of market funds in which the contributions were invested) ☐ Yes ☐ No

   ii. If still working, at what age will you be able to retire with full pension? _____

   iii. Approx. how much annual pension earnings will you be able to draw? $ _____

      a. Is your monthly pension income reduced if you retire early? ☐ Yes ☐ No

      b. If yes, by how much (please verify for your own peace of mind)? _____

C. Registered Tax-Deferred Retirement Savings

1. Do you have investments in a 401K, RRSP, or similar plan? ☐ Yes ☐ No

   i. If yes, what is the approximate value at this time? $ _____

   ii. Based on current interest rates and inflation, what % can you withdraw *annually* without depleting the principal amount prematurely? _____

2. Have you sought tax planning advice on the optimal strategy for drawing income in your post-retirement years? ☐ Yes ☐ No

   i. If Yes, Congratulations!

   ii. If No, this is highly recommended and may be the best investment you can make – the cost of the advice may be a fraction of the taxes paid if you do not plan prudently and early (preferably while still in your earning years).

NOTES

V. Life Insurance:

A. Do you have life insurance? ☐ Yes ☐ No

    1. If yes, at what age does your coverage expire? _____

    2. What is the total value of your life insurance policy? $ _____

    3. Are you able to renew without a medical checkup? ☐ Yes ☐ No

        i. If yes, is there a substantial increase in premium? ☐ Yes ☐ No

            a. Are you currently enjoying good health? ☐ Yes ☐ No

            b. If No, will your partner have other income to support them if your insurance expires before you pass? ☐ Yes ☐ No

B. Have you put a "safety net" in place for your partner's "Next Chapter" security (i.e., without you and your retirement income being available)? ☐ Yes ☐ No

    1. Have you and your partner discussed what the other will do when one of you passes? ☐ Yes ☐ No

    2. If No, do you believe this is an important conversation to have? ☐ Yes ☐ No

NOTES

VI. Other *Monthly* Income (from all sources)

A. Federal pension earnings:
    1. Social Security (US only) $ _____
    2. Canada Pension (Cdn only)
        i. CPP $ _____
        ii. OAS $ _____
        iii. GIS $ _____
    3. Disability pension earnings $ _____
    4. Other gov't pension earnings $ _____

B. Employer pension earnings:
    1. Primary employer pension plan $ _____
    2. Other employer pension plans $ _____

C. Other earnings (from all sources):
    1. Dividend earnings $ _____
    2. _____ $ _____
    3. _____ $ _____
    4. _____ $ _____
    5. _____ $ _____

D. Potential annual withdrawal of invested retirement savings:
    1. Registered pension earnings:
        i. 401k or other plans (US only) $ _____
        ii. RRSP (Cdn only) $ _____
        iii. RRIF (Cdn only) $ _____
        iv. GIC (Cdn only) $ _____
        v. Treasury Bills (T-Bills) $ _____
        vi. Bonds $ _____
        vii. Annuity:
            1. _____ $ _____
            2. _____ $ _____
        viii. Other:
            1. _____ $ _____
            2. _____ $ _____

E. Total Annual Income (from all sources) $ _____
    1. Estimated income tax $ _____

Net Annual Income $ _____

NOTES

In Summary:

Congratulations!

For each of us, the determination of "How Much is Enough" is a personal choice. However, in order to make quality decisions in life, it is crucial that those decisions are based on sound information.

This exercise is intended to stimulate each participant's thought process about their financial resources. By planning accordingly, we can optimize our "Next Chapter" lifestyle and realize as many of our Bucket List aspirations as possible.

> CHOICE, NOT CHANCE,
> DETERMINES EVERYTHING
> THAT HAPPENS IN OUR FUTURE.

With this information and input from your financial planner in hand, your Downsizing Plan is taking shape. To help you pull all the elements of your personal Downsizing Plan together, your Real Estate & Downsizing Coach can be an invaluable objective resource. As these special people tend to exhibit endless patience, maturity, and first-hand personal midlife experience, they are ready to work with you to translate the information you have gathered through your Downsizing Assessment process into a "Next Chapter" plan.

If you would like assistance in connecting with a *qualified Real Estate & Downsizing Coach* in your area, please go to www.TheBookOnDownsizing.com and select "Contact Us".

NOTES

Part B

The purpose of this section is to ensure that you and your partner are "on the same page" with regard to your financial position and direction.

<u>Monthly Income and Expense Summary</u>

Enter your total monthly income from all sources

_____

Deduct Home Expenses

Mortgage or Rent Payment

Property Taxes (monthly amount)

Utilities (heat, hydro, water and/or maintenance fee if condo)

Insurance Premium (property, life)

Credit Line/loan payments

Sub-Total : Net Balance after Home Expenses

Deduct Other Monthly Expenses

Phone & Cable costs

Vehicle operating costs (Insurance, gas, oil, repair,)

Vehicle loan/lease payment

Food costs

Credit Card payments

Clothing expenditures (average)

Entertainment costs (dining, theatre, etc)

Other Credit Line/loan payments

Sub-Total : Monthly Net Balance after expenses

Annualized cash available: (monthly net balance x 12 months)

How do you want to spend/invest the annualized cash available?

NOTES

Part C

My Downsizing Asset Calculation

The Book on Downsizing has been designed to help you and your partner discover how much value there is in the real estate, vehicles, toys and other "stuff" you currently own.

Feedback from those who have completed this process ranges from "WOW! I didn't realize how much net worth I really have" to "Oh my gosh, I can't believe how little value is left in all the vehicles in our personal *fleet*." This exercise helps each partner answer the often unspoken question that holds us back from "moving on"... and that is, "How much is enough?"

"RAPIDLY DEPRECIATING ASSETS CAN HAVE A SIGNIFICANT IMPACT ON AVAILABLE RETIREMENT RESOURCES AND OUR FUTURE QUALITY OF LIFE"

To get the most from this exercise, we recommend that you utilize the knowledge and skills of your Real Estate & Downsizing Coach, who can provide you with a comparative market analysis that will assist you in valuing each of your real estate assets.

To estimate the value of your business, your coach may be able to refer a qualified realtor who specializes in this area. In order to obtain a realistic valuation, this should include factors such as buildings, inventory, equipment, receivables, and other less tangible assets. While this may involve considerable time and research, any cost associated with this process is typically money well invested.

"TAKING INVENTORY ALLOWS US TO SEE WHAT WE HAVE ACCUMULATED AND TO KEEP ONLY WHAT FITS OUR "NEXT CHAPTER" LIFESTYLE"

As we suggest in *The Book on Downsizing*, there are several objective sources that can assist you in determining the value of your vehicles and toys. In this area, it is particularly important to be conservative, as depreciation is the invisible thief that erodes the investment, often well before we have sufficiently enjoyed it or worn it out. Regardless, the price someone would be willing to pay us for the vehicle today is the best indicator of current value.

The Chattels category includes items such as furniture, appliances, art, jewelry, and heirlooms. These are often difficult to value, since items such as appliances depreciate more quickly than we would hope, while furniture and heirlooms are less valued by our children and grandchildren (typically Generation X and Y). Our art and jewelry also tends to have less value than we may have hoped, and certainly less that we may have been led to believe when we *"invested"* in it.

We encourage you to have fun with this process. It can be both enlightening and freeing as you determine what is important in planning for your "Next Chapter" lifestyle.

NOTES

Assets We Currently Own (in estimating value, be conservative, as this is for your planning purposes only)

A. Appreciating Assets:

  1. Residences:

    a. Principal Home – Location: _____ Value $ _____

    b. Alternate Home – Location: _____ Value $ _____

  2. Waterfront/Waterside property - Location: _____ Value $ _____

  3. Country Property – Location: _____ Value $ _____

  4. Winter home (outside Canada) – Location: _____ Value $ _____

  5. Condo in the city (weekend getaway) – Location: _____ Value $ _____

  6. Investment properties:

    a. Location: _____ Value $ _____

    b. Location: _____ Value $ _____

    c. Location: _____ Value $ _____

  7. Farm - Location: _____ Value $ _____

  8. Other: _____ Location: _____ Value $ _____

  9. Other: _____ Location: _____ Value $ _____

B. Depreciating Assets

  1. Cars:

    a. Make:_____ Year:_____ Est. Value:_____

    b. Make:_____ Year:_____ Est. Value:_____

    c. Make:_____ Year:_____ Est. Value:_____

  2. Trucks:

    a. Make:_____ Year:_____ Est. Value:_____

    b. Make:_____ Year:_____ Est. Value:_____

NOTES

3. Vintage vehicles:

    a. Make:_____ Year:_____ Est. Value:_____

    b. Make:_____ Year:_____ Est. Value:_____

    c. Make:_____ Year:_____ Est. Value:_____

4. Large boats:

    a. Make:_____ Year:_____ Est. Value:_____

    b. Make:_____ Year:_____ Est. Value:_____

5. Motor Home / House Trailer:

    a. Make:_____ Year:_____ Est. Value:_____

6. Motorcycles:

    a. Make:_____ Year:_____ Est. Value:_____

    b. Make:_____ Year:_____ Est. Value:_____

7. Snowmobiles:

    a. Make:_____ Year:_____ Est. Value:_____

    b. Make:_____ Year:_____ Est. Value:_____

8. Jet Skis:

    a. Make:_____ Year:_____ Est. Value:_____

    b. Make:_____ Year:_____ Est. Value:_____

9. ATVs:

    a. Make:_____ Year:_____ Est. Value:_____

    b. Make:_____ Year:_____ Est. Value:_____

10. Smaller Boats / Runabouts < 20':

    a. Make:_____ Year:_____ Est. Value:_____

11. Other:

    a. Make:_____ Year:_____ Est. Value:_____

    b. Make:_____ Year:_____ Est. Value:_____

NOTES

C. Chattels:

1. Furniture:

   a. Dining Room Suite - Approx. Age _____ Est. Value: _____

   b. _____ - Approx. Age _____ Est. Value: _____

   c. _____ - Approx. Age _____ Est. Value: _____

   d. _____ - Approx. Age _____ Est. Value: _____

2. Appliances:

   a. Kitchen (major appliances only)

      i. _____ Age _ Original Cost _____ Est Value _____

      ii. _____ Age _ Original Cost _____ Est Value _____

      iii. _____ Age _ Original Cost _____ Est Value _____

      iv. _____ _ Original Cost _____ Est Value _____

   b. Other:

      i. _____ Age _ Original Cost _____ Est Value _____

      ii. _____ Age _ Original Cost _____ Est Value _____

      iii. _____ Age _ Original Cost _____ Est Value _____

3. Art:

   a. Size: ____ x ____ Artist: _____ Est Value _____

   b. Size: ____ x ____ Artist: _____ Est Value _____

   c. Size: ____ x ____ Artist: _____ Est Value _____

4. Jewelry:

   a. Item: _____ Age: _____ Est Value _____

   b. Item: _____ Age: _____ Est Value _____

   c. Item: _____ Age: _____ Est Value _____

5. Heirlooms and Antiques:

   a. _____ Age _____ Est Value _____

   b. _____ Age _____ Est Value _____

   c. _____ Age _____ Est Value _____

   d. _____ Age _____ Est Value _____

NOTES

In Summary – My Downsizing Asset Calculation:

Congratulations on completing this self-assessment of your assets.

This exercise tends to be one of the most difficult, as it requires us to assess the current value of the major items we own. As the process of downsizing can free us for the adventures of the Next Chapter, by conservatively valuing each of these, it can be helpful in choosing to "let them go."

> "MOVING INTO YOUR "NEXT CHAPTER" HOME UNENCUMBERED BY 'STUFF' GIVES YOU THE FREEDOM TO DESIGN THE REST OF YOUR LIFE"

When you meet with your Real Estate & Downsizing Coach, the above information will assist in reviewing the comparative market assessment for your appreciating real estate assets, as well as the estimated current value of your vehicles and chattels. This summary can be a valuable component in determining your overall "Next Chapter" financial position.

If you would like assistance in connecting with a *qualified Real Estate & Downsizing Coach* in your area, please go to www.TheBookOnDownsizing.com and select "Contact Us".

NOTES

Part D

Other Downsizing Home Alternatives

Many Downsizers are hoping the equity in their current home will be enough to supplement their federal pension earnings in retirement. However if a company pension, retirement savings, investments and/or personal savings are insufficient to support the lifestyle they had planned, cashing in on their home may not be the right strategy.

> "SELLING OUR CURRENT HOME AND RENTING SHOULD ONLY BE CONSIDERED AFTER CAREFUL ANALYSIS OF ALL YOUR OPTIONS"

One of the options Downsizers in this position may be considering is selling their home and renting an apartment. While this seems like a viable solution on the surface, the following calculation will help to determine if this strategy will be ideal for them.

Is Selling Our Current Home and Renting an Apartment a Viable Option for Us?

For the purposes of this calculation, we are using a 10-year planning window. If you are in good health, then, based on today's normal life expectancy, you may alter the calculation to cover whatever planning period you deem appropriate for your circumstances. To complete this exercise, you will need to gather the following information:

a) Determine the monthly cost to rent a modest apartment that is large enough to meet your needs.

b) Estimate the cost of major purchases you anticipate making over the next 10 years – e.g., a new vehicle every five years, annual vacations, health and other insurances, gifting.

c) Determine your monthly budget for living expenses – food, clothing, household supplies.

d) Calculate total income from pensions and all other sources.

e) Based on your annual income (from all sources), estimate income tax owed.

This exercise will provide a financial snapshot of how viable this approach is for you and your partner. However, before considering this as your strategy, we recommend that you spend some time checking out the rental apartment lifestyle so there are no surprises later on.

"Purpose-built" rental apartments are buildings that were specifically built to be rented and provide no option for home ownership. While many of these buildings are older, some have been well maintained and provide the benefit of being available on a long-term basis. The lifestyle in these rental apartment buildings is typically quite different, however, and you may not find it appealing on a social or emotional level if you have been a homeowner for many years.

The other option is to rent a home, townhome or condo suite. While this provides many of the comforts you enjoyed as a homeowner, the owner may chose to sell the property, requiring you to move every year or two.

NOTES

This exercise highlights the importance of completing your Downsizing Plan as early as possible. For some, it will be quite revealing, particularly if it reveals that there is not enough annual income, including the residual equity left in your home, to support your anticipated annual expenditures on a longer-term basis.

While this will not be the case for most Downsizers, what if this is your situation? In her recent book *Never Too Late*, author Gail Vaz-Oxlade provides a no-nonsense approach for people of any age to take charge of their financial situation and start planning appropriately for retirement, now.

> "LIFE HAPPENS, BUT IT'S NEVER TOO LATE TO FACE REALITY, ADAPT TO CHANGE, AND COMMIT TO LIVING DIFFERENTLY"

The most important thing to remember is that we have the *choice* to act now and take control of our future. If we do nothing, others will make choices for us that may be less appealing.

By completing the following mini-budget for ongoing living costs associated with a rental property, you will be able to evaluate if selling your home and renting is advisable for you. Reviewing this information with your Real Estate & Downsizing Coach may be helpful, as they can often suggest alternative lifestyle options that could work even better for you and your partner.

NOTES

Part E
Downsizers' Sell-n-Rent Calculation:

Monthly Income
_____

Monthly Living Costs
Apartment / Condo Rental - _____
Parking Cost - _____
Heat (Where Applicable) - _____
Electricity (Where Applicable) - _____
Phone, Cable & Internet - _____

Insurance
Auto,Tenant & Life - _____

Transportation
Vehicle Purchase - _____
Fuel & Maintenance - _____
Transit (Bus,Taxi etc) - _____

Personal Expenses
Food - _____
Clothing - _____
Household Supplies - _____
Healthcare - _____
Entertainment - _____

Other
1. _____ - _____
2. _____ - _____
3. _____ - _____

Total
[   ]

Is selling your home and renting a viable option for you?

NOTES

6

My Downsizing Home Profile

Part A

Profiling Your Next Chapter Home Preferences

Whether positive or negative, fulfilling or empty, your lifestyle and the house you reside in are closely linked, and your home is a reflection of how you and your partner see the world.

The following questions will assist you in defining your ideal home, and identifying the features that are most appealing to you. Your responses, when compared with those of your partner, will enable you to foster the compatible shared lifestyle you both look forward to creating in this next home.

"A HOME IS THE RELATIONSHIP BETWEEN THE STRUCTURE YOU LIVE IN AND THE LIFE THAT YOU LIVE IN IT"

A. My preferred type of Next Chapter home would be: Rate these on a scale of 1 to 10, where 10 is most important)

   1. Detached ☐

   2. Semi-Detached ☐

   3. Townhome – Freehold ☐

   4. Townhome – Condo ☐

   5. Apartment – Condo ☐

B. My preferred style of Next Chapter home would be: (Rate these on a scale of 1 to 10, where 10 is most important)

   1. Bungalow or Ranch (no steps on main floor level) ☐

   2. Raised Bungalow or Raised Ranch (several steps from foyer to main floor level) ☐

NOTES

3. Multi-Level:

    i.   Side Split ☐

    ii. Back Split ☐

4. 2-Story ☐

5. 1 ½-Story ☐

6. 2 ½-Story ☐

C. My preferred basement-level features are: (Rate these on a scale of 1 to 10, where 10 is most important)

    1. Unfinished basement is ideal – for storage only ☐

    2. Unfinished basement preferred – wish to finish to own taste ☐

    3. Finished basement preferred ☐

    4. Walkout basement (sloping lot with grade-level walkout at front or rear) ☐

    5. Walk-up basement (with stairs to garage or outside, as well as to the main floor) ☐

D. The ideal location for my Next Chapter home is: (Rate these on a scale of 1 to 10, where 10 is most important)

    1. Downtown ☐

    2. Suburban neighborhood ☐

    3. Waterfront or waterside ☐

    4. Close to transportation (e.g., subway or bus stop) ☐

    5. Countryside ☐

    6. Small village or town ☐

    7. Adult lifestyle community ☐

    8. Other: ☐ _____

E. Acceptable travel time to services (shopping, hospital, pharmacy, restaurants, entertainment, etc.) is: Rate these on a scale of 1 to 10, where 10 is most important)

    1. Walking distance ☐

    2. 5 minutes ☐ .

    3. 15 minutes ☐

NOTES

4. 30 minutes ☐

5. 45 minutes ☐

6. 1 hour or more ☐

F. The full-time residents in my Next Chapter home will be:

1. Me ☐

2. Me and my spouse/partner ☐

3. Me, my spouse/partner, and a dependent person ☐

4. Me, my spouse/partner, plus multiple family members (extended family home) ☐

5. Other: _____

G. The number of bedrooms used more than once a month will be:

1. 1 ☐

2. 2 ☐

3. 3 ☐

4. 4 or more ☐

5. On average, we expect guests to be staying with us _____ nights per month

H. The number of bathrooms used more than twice a day will be:

1. 1 ☐

2. 2 ☐

3. 3 ☐

4. 4 or more ☐

I. The bathroom features I value most are: (Rate these on a scale of 1 to 10, where 10 is most important)

1. Ensuite bathroom ☐

2. Semi-ensuite bathroom ☐

3. Soaker tub ☐

4. Step-in shower (low threshold) ☐

5. One-piece tub and shower (easy to clean and maintain) ☐

NOTES

6. Double sinks (i.e., two wash basins) ☐

7. Window for natural light ☐

8. Bathroom features are really not very important to me ☐

9. Other: _____

J. The 10 items in my current home that mean the most to me and need to have a place in my Next Chapter home (e.g., furniture, appliances, art, and accessories - e.g. treadmill) in order of importance are:

1. _____ Importance: _____

2. _____ Importance: _____

3. _____ Importance: _____

4. _____ Importance: _____

5. _____ Importance: _____

6. _____ Importance: _____

7. _____ Importance: _____

8. _____ Importance: _____

9. _____ Importance: _____

10. _____ Importance: _____

In Summary – Profiling Your Next Chapter Home:

Congratulations!

We hope this helps to foster dialogue between you and your spouse or partner, and assists you to develop a shared vision of your next home. Your next step is to fill out "My Envisioned Next Chapter Home" assessment.

Your Real Estate & Downsizing Coach can be invaluable in answering questions and providing additional information as you go through the process of evaluating the most important features of your "Next Chapter" home.

If you would like assistance in finding a *qualified Real Estate & Downsizing Coach* in your area, please go to www.TheBookOnDownsizing.com and select "Contact Us".

NOTES

Part B

The Home Of Your Dreams

My Envisioned Next Chapter Home

We're now ready to start exploring the particulars of your ideal downsized home. Although most of us would say we live in a nice house now, many would also confide that it wasn't really exactly what we wanted when we purchased it. At the time, it "fit our budget" or "it was close to the right schools," or perhaps "it was near work so we only needed one car."

Every weekend, across the country, open houses are inundated with graying Baby Boomers looking for that "perfect home." When asked to describe it, many simply say, "I'll know it when I see it!" Sadly, for many of these people, the dream goes unfulfilled because they don't have a plan and really don't know what they want. Too often, when they do find it, they may suddenly realize that it's not affordable.

> "OUR HOME AND OUR CONNECTION TO IT HAVE A PROFOUND IMPACT ON OUR CREATIVITY, OUR RESILIENCE, AND OUR ENDURING PASSION FOR LIFE"

Envision a Day in Your New Home

By imagining a complete day in your new home and experiencing your daily routine in new surroundings, you can begin to clarify what's important to you and take the first step in making your dream a reality.

If you have trouble with the concept of visualizing, you can cut out pictures from magazines or new home brochures, or print images you've seen online. Collect these in a scrapbook and, as you flip through them, a picture will begin to form of the type of environment that resonates with you.

Get a notebook that can serve as your "Home Journal." Start a page entitled "My new home feels like…" and then describe the feeling as you walk in through the front door.

> "YOUR JOURNAL CAN BE A MAGICAL TOOL IN SHAPING THE VISION OF YOUR "NEXT CHAPTER" HOME, ONE CREATIVE THOUGHT AT A TIME"

What do you see around you? Does it feel spacious and open, or intimate and cozy? Does it feel serene and peaceful, or is it full of light with lots of windows? Are there hardwood floors or broadloom? Is there a family room and, if so, what is it like (e.g., does it have a fireplace)?

Envision yourself wandering through each room, and make notes as you go.

Now, on a separate page in your journal, walk through and describe how your current home feels, room by room. Be sure to note what you love about each room, as well as what you would change if you could.

By going through this room-by-room process, you will be able to identify how many rooms you actually need and will be prepared to clean. You will also become more motivated to "let go" of those things that don't appear in your vision of the future.

NOTES

Notes

Notes

NOTES

NOTES

Bringing Your Rooms to Life

Using your mental picture, or the photos you found, you can now begin to furnish your rooms. First, we'll place each of those 10 "must keep" items into its respective room in your new home.

Using a piece of graph paper, draw each furniture piece to scale, label it, and cut it out. Then, draw each of the other items you plan to place in your rooms and cut them out as well.

Next, on another piece of graph paper, place each of these furniture "cut-outs" to determine how large the room needs to be to accommodate them.

Go through your downsized home, room-by-room, completing this process for each room and documenting the ideal room measurements. This will provide your first concrete information on how large your next home needs to be.

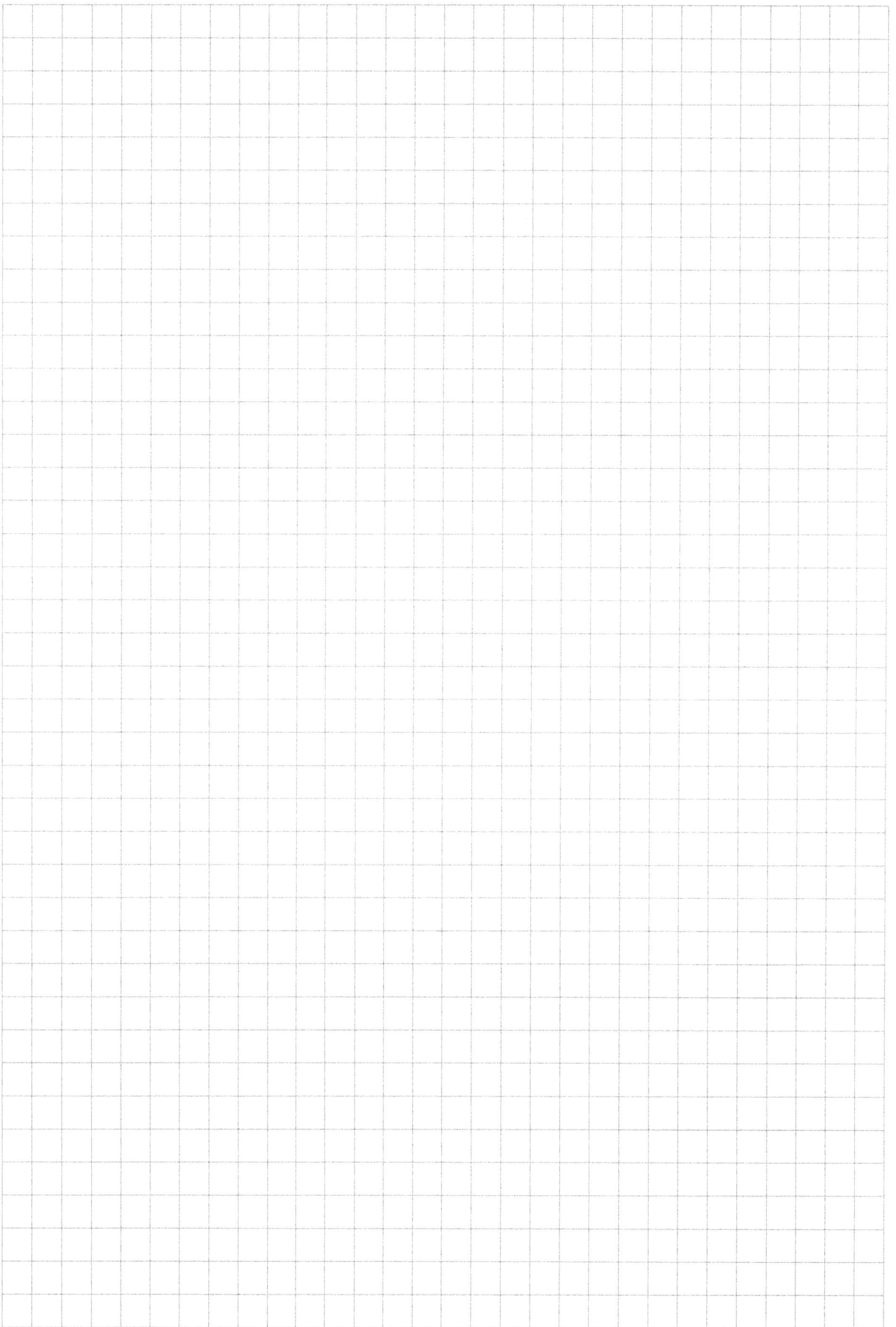

Defining Your Envisioned "Next Chapter" Home:

The following exercise has been designed to assist you in identifying those features that will define your "Next Chapter" home. By prioritizing your choices for each aspect of this home, you are building a profile that gives you and your partner clarity on your wants and wishes. Based on the profile generated by this exercise, you can develop a shared vision of the right features.

After developing your envisioned home profile with your partner, you can then meet with your Real Estate & Downsizing Coach to determine if homes of this type could be available in your neighborhood of choice where you'd most like your "Next Chapter" home to be. While the home you envisioned may not exist in your preferred community, your home profile will enable your coach to provide you with options and alternatives to evaluate.

> "SEASONED DOWNSIZERS SAY THAT IF THEY WERE TO DO IT AGAIN, THEY'D DESIGN THEIR "NEXT CHAPTER" HOME FOR THE TWO PEOPLE WHO LIVE THERE 365 DAYS A YEAR"

We hope you'll enjoy envisioning the "Next Chapter" home you'll love to live in. Please rate each choice on a scale of 1 to 10 (where 10 = most important).

I. The overall feeling as we walk through our "Next Chapter" home is:

A. Bright, airy and alive ☐

B. Serene, tranquil and peaceful ☐

C. Open concept and free-flowing ☐

D. Intimate, with several "personal spaces" – den, living room, family room ☐

E. Traditional - lots of natural wood and detailing (crown molding, trim) ☐

F. Contemporary – decor, kitchen, baths, trim ☐

G. Other:

    1. _____

    2. _____

    3. _____

Notes

II. When we step through the door to the backyard, the experience we envision is: Rate these (1 to 10) 10 = most important:

A. Sunny, open, ideal for my vegetable and flower gardens ☐

B. Shaded and cool ☐

C. Fenced ☐

D. Lots of privacy (screening, bushes) ☐

E. Open, with ample access to interact with neighbors ☐

F. Flat ☐

G. Sloping ☐

H. Terraced ☐

I. Low-maintenance is a priority ☐

J. The backyard is not important ☐

K. Other: _____

III. When we stand on our deck or patio, we prefer to look out onto: Rate these on a scale of (1 to 10) 10 = most important:

A. Woods ☐

B. Park ☐

C. Open field ☐

D. Not very important to me ☐

E. Other:

1. _____

2. _____

NOTES

IV. A water feature is important to us in our "Next Chapter" home: Rate these on a scale of (1 to 10) 10 = most important:

A. Swimming Pool ☐

B. Hot Tub ☐

C. Pond ☐

D. Fountain ☐

E. Other:

    1. _____

    2. _____

    3. _____

V. As we look around, the landscaping and gardens we would prefer include: Rate these (1 to 10) 10 = most important:

A. Open lawns, no gardens or bushes to maintain ☐

B. Perimeter gardens and perennials that can be nurtured ☐

C. Lots of evergreens (conifers) and bushes in the yard (low-maintenance) ☐

D. Shade trees – three-season enjoyment with annual fall leaf cleanup ☐

E. Not very important to me ☐

F. Other:

    1. _____

    2. _____

    3. _____

NOTES

VI. When we stand in front of our "Next Chapter" home and look around, we prefer: (i.e. the neighboring houses around you) Rate these (1 to 10) 10 = most important:

A. A front porch ☐

B. No sidewalk in front of our home (i.e., on our side of the street) ☐

C. Mature trees on the street ☐

D. The houses nearby are similar to our home ☐

E. The houses nearby are different from our home ☐

F. The street is relatively quiet with few cars going by ☐

G. Lots of people walking (provides an opportunity to socialize) ☐

H. Not very important to me ☐

I. Other: _____

J. _____

VII. The garage and driveway of our home: Rate these (1 to 10) 10 = most important:

A. Currently we have the following vehicles to park at our "Next Chapter" home:

    1. Cars   Qty _____ Importance ☐

    2. Trucks   Qty _____ Importance ☐

    3. Motorcycles   Qty _____ Importance ☐

    4. Other: _____ Qty _____ Importance ☐

B. The garage I would like to have is: Rate these (1 to 10) 10 = most important:

    1. Single ☐

    2. Double ☐

    3. Three-car or more ☐

    4. Not very important to me ☐

Notes

C. The driveway is:

1. Single ☐

2. Double ☐

3. Oversized ☐

4. Not very important to me ☐

VIII. Driving through the neighborhood: (Rate these items on a scale of (1 to 10) 10 = most important:

A. As we back out of the driveway and start down the street, the homes are:

1. newer (less than 20 years) ☐

2. older (21 – 50 years) ☐

3. quite old (more than 50 years) ☐

4. Not very important to me ☐

B. There are many stop signs, streetlights, or traffic lights ☐

C. There are stores and shopping nearby ☐

D. There are restaurants close by (within 4- 8 blocks, i.e.., walking distance) ☐

E. There is a school, library, community center, or place of worship nearby ☐

F. The people you pass on the street are:

1. Our age ☐

2. Younger ☐

3. Older ☐

G. Are people walking or does everyone travel in their cars _____

H. Other: _____

I. Not very important to me ☐

NOTES

IX. Determining the size and layout of our ideal home: Rate these (1 to 10) 10 = most important:

A. The most important rooms in our "Next Chapter" home are:

1. Formal Living Room (Parlor) ☐

2. Dining Room ☐

3. Eat-In Kitchen (i.e., room for table and at least 2 chairs) ☐

4. Breakfast Room or Nook (typically overlooking yard) ☐

5. Family Room (typically on the main floor) ☐

6. Spacious Master Bedroom with Walk-In Closet ☐

7. Ensuite Bathroom with Spa or Soaker Tub & Shower ☐

8. Guest Room or combined 2nd Bedroom & Office ☐

9. Finished areas in the basement:

   a. Games ☐

   b. Sitting ☐

   c. Computer area ☐

   d. Home theatre ☐

   e. Office ☐

   f. Bedroom(s) ☐

B. Entertaining and Hosting: Rate these (1 to 10) 10 = most important:

1. Our typical overnight guests will typically be:

   a. Children ☐

   b. Grandchildren ☐

   c. Siblings ☐

   d. Older Relatives ☐

   e. Friends ☐

   f. International Guests ☐

NOTES

2. Overnight Guest Details:

    a. How many nights per year would you typically host overnight guests? ☐

    b. How many guests do you typically host at one time? ☐

    c. How long do your overnight guests typically stay? ☐

    d. How many nights per month would you typically host children's sleepovers at your home? ☐

C. Preferred Entertaining Events: - Rate these (1 to 10) 10 = most important:

    1. Formal Dinner Parties ☐

    2. Casual Dining & BBQs ☐

    3. Movie Nights ☐

    4. Holiday Gatherings (including Christmas) hosted at our house ☐

D. Hosting preference: - Rate these (1 to 10) 10 = most important:

    1. Serve formal dinner in dining room ☐

    2. Informal dining in breakfast room or eat-in kitchen ☐

    3. Casual dining for 1 or 2 at breakfast bar ☐

    4. Outdoor dining on deck or patio (in season) ☐

E. Rooms in our home that will be required most frequently for entertaining and hosting: - Rate these (1 to 10) 10 = most important:

    1. Living Room ☐

    2. Dining Room ☐

    3. Family Room ☐

    4. Breakfast Room ☐

    5. Deck or Patio ☐

    6. Guest Room ☐

    7. Recreation Room ☐

    8. Other: _____

NOTES

F. Kitchen preferences - Rate these (1 to 10) 10 = most important

1. Bright and airy ☐

2. Intimate and cozy ☐

3. Galley-style ☐

4. Open to breakfast room ☐

5. Open to family room ☐

6. Breakfast bar ☐

7. Eat-in kitchen (accommodates small table and chairs) ☐

8. Adjoining breakfast room ☐

9. Walkout to patio or deck ☐

10. Updated appointments:

  a. New kitchen cabinets ☐

  b. Granite (or similar) countertops ☐

  c. Range:

    i. Gas ☐

    ii. Electric ☐

  d. Built-in microwave ☐

  e. Tiled backsplash ☐

  f. Kitchen storage (for roasting pans, stock pots, bread maker, etc.):

    i. Pot & Pan Drawers ☐

    ii. Pantry ☐

NOTES

X. Decor elements that are important to us: - Rate these (1 to 10) 10 = most important

    A. Wall covering ☐

    B. 9' ceilings ☐

    C. Hardwood flooring ☐

    D. Laminate flooring ☐

    E. Ceramic tile ☐

    F. Ceiling fans ☐

    G. Lighting preferences:

        1. Pot lighting ☐

        2. Track lighting ☐

        3. Contemporary style fixtures ☐

        4. Traditional style fixtures ☐

        5. Under-cabinet lighting ☐

        6. Indirect Lighting ☐

XI. Other features that we enjoy - Rate these (1 to 10) 10 = most important:

    A. Fireplace:

        1. Gas ☐

        2. Woodburning ☐

    B. Main Floor Master Bedroom ☐

    C. Main Floor Laundry ☐

    D. Main Floor Powder Room ☐

    E. Inside Entry from Garage ☐

    F. Alarm System ☐

    G. Home Theatre-wired ☐

    H. High Speed Internet ☐

    I. Patio or Garden Door walkout to deck or patio ☐

NOTES

XII. Heating & Air Conditioning - Rate these (1 to 10) 10 = most important

A. Forced Air:
1. Gas ☐
2. Oil ☐
3. Electric ☐

B. Heat Pump
1. Ground Source (typically country properties only) ☐
2. Air source ☐

C. Hot-water Radiators ☐

D. In-floor Radiant Heating ☐

E. Heat Recovery Ventilation System (HRV) ☐

F. HEPA filter (pollen & dust removal) ☐

G. Furnace-mounted Electronic Humidifier ☐

H. Air Conditioner Systems:
1. Forced Air Furnace-mounted Central Air Conditioning ☐
2. Hi-wall A/C units with Heat Pump (where forced air ducts are unavailable) ☐
3. Window air conditioning units ☐

XIII. Home upgrades already done (typically on homes 20 years and older) - Rate these (1 to 10) 10 = most important

A. Roofing shingles ☐

B. Aluminum eaves troughs, soffits, and fascia ☐

C. Windows ☐

D. Exterior doors:
1. Front door system ☐
2. Patio or garden door ☐
3. Garage doors ☐
4. Side entrance (where applicable) ☐
5. Skylights ☐

Notes

E. Interior doors and hardware ☐

F. Closet doors ☐

G. Bathroom fixtures ☐

H. Bathroom vanity and hardware ☐

I. Flooring ☐

XIV. Maintaining our next home: (check those that apply)

A. I enjoy working on my home and gardens:

1. More than 6 hours / week ☐

2. 3 – 6 hours / week ☐

3. I do not enjoy doing work and prefer condo lifestyle ☐

4. I want someone to manage all exterior maintenance around our home ☐

B. I enjoy home maintenance and typically do the following: (Check those that apply)

1. Window cleaning ☐

2. Painting ☐

3. Cleaning gutters ☐

4. Mowing lawn ☐

5. Trimming shrubs and pruning trees ☐

6. Snow removal (where applicable) ☐

7. I don't enjoy these tasks and contract them to others ☐

XV. Storage space preferences: - Rate these (1 to 10) 10 = most important

A. Closets ☐

B. Basement ☐

C. Garage mezzanine ☐

D. Attic ☐

E. Garden shed ☐

F. Off-site self-storage ☐

NOTES

In Summary – Bring your Envisioned "Next Chapter" Home to Life:

Congratulations!

This exercise has been designed to assist you in identifying those features that will define your "Next Chapter" home. By prioritizing your choices for each aspect of this home, you are building a profile that gives you and your partner clarity on your wants and wishes. We hope the profile generated by this exercise will foster ongoing dialogue with your spouse or partner and assist you in developing that shared vision of the ideal features for your next home.

"SMALLER, FEWER OR LESS DOESN'T HAVE TO MEAN INFERIOR – HAVE FUN AND "THINK OUTSIDE THE BOX" TO OPTIMIZE YOUR "NEXT CHAPTER" LIVING SPACES"

Your Real Estate & Downsizing Coach can now assist you in determining if homes of this type could be available in the neighborhood where you'd most like your "Next Chapter" home to be. While the home you envisioned may not exist in your preferred community, your home profile will enable your coach to provide you with options and other alternatives to evaluate.

If you would like assistance in connecting with a *qualified Real Estate & Downsizing Coach* in your area, please go to www.TheBookOnDownsizing.com and select "Contact Us".

NOTES

7

Creating My "Bucket List"

In the movie *The Bucket List,* Jack Nicholson and Morgan Freeman portray two terminally ill men who deal with their situation by making a list on a sheet of paper of "unfulfilled life dreams" and then go off to realize them. This exercise can be extremely valuable for Baby Boomers, as well as, their younger peers.

When we are young, we all think we are ten feet tall and invincible. Then one day, life throws us a curve that we did not expect. Life is unpredictable and we shouldn't wait until tomorrow to explore our dreams and aspirations. By writing them down, we acknowledge them and make them real for us.

"YOUR JOURNEY OF A LIFETIME BEGINS WITH THE SEED OF AN IDEA, WATERED WITH COMMITMENT, AND MADE A REALITY WITH CAREFUL PLANNING"

The following questions are designed to help you reconnect with your dreams and create your Bucket List. When you finish, you can generate your list and prioritize it, based on where you are in your life today and your capacity to physically achieve your goals.

You may even discover that just doing research for some items is enough to satisfy your desire. For example, if you muse about what it would be like to walk along Bourbon Street in New Orleans, you can go there virtually (e.g., via http://showmystreet.com/) and decide if it is really important to you before making it a high-priority item on your list. When it comes to defining the Next Chapter of your life and the events that will shape it, the Internet can be your window to a world that wasn't available to any generation before ours. If you are familiar with Google, then you know how easy it is to research virtually anything.

If working with a computer is not your thing, you may have to rely on your partner, your children, or a good friend to facilitate this exercise. We sincerely hope you will commit to identifying these aspirations and making a list. Simply by acknowledging them, you can have a profound impact in making them happen.

"MAKE MEMORIES, NOT REGRETS..."

To make the process easier, we have divided the questions into five general categories to help you discover your unfulfilled dreams and aspirations:

    I.   People
    II. Places
    III. Events
    IV. Experiences
    V. Activities

Notes

I. People:

A. The person in the world I would most like to meet is: _____

    1   I would like to meet this person because: _____

    2. The one question I would like to ask is: _____

    3. On a scale of 1 – 10 (10 being highest), this person would be # _____ on my list

Pose Question: "Is there another inspiring or interesting person you would like to meet?" ☐ Yes ☐ No

If Yes – Who would that be? _____

Make a list of the next people I would most like to meet in priority sequence.
    If No – go to next category: "**Places**"

B. The next person in the world I would most like to meet is: _____

    1   I would like to meet this person because: _____

    2. The one question I would like to ask is: _____

    3. On a scale of 1 – 10 (10 being highest), this person would be # _____ on my list

C. The next person in the world I would most like to meet is: _____

    1   I would like to meet this person because: _____

    2. The one question I would like to ask is: _____

    3. On a scale of 1 – 10 (10 being highest), this person would be # _____ on my list

D. The next person in the world I would most like to meet is: _____

    1   I would like to meet this person because: _____

    2. The one question I would like to ask is: _____

    3. On a scale of 1 – 10 (10 being highest), this person would be # _____ on my list

E. The next person in the world I would most like to meet is: _____

    1   I would like to meet this person because: _____

    2. The one question I would like to ask is: _____

    3. On a scale of 1 – 10 (10 being highest), this person would be # _____ on my list

Notes

II. Places:

A. The place in the world I would most like to visit is: _____

    1. I would like to go there because: _____

    2. The top 3 things I would like to see there are:

        a. _____

        b. _____

        c. _____

    3. On a scale of 1 -10 (10 being most interesting) I would rank this place # _____

Pose Question: "Is there another interesting or exciting place you would like to visit?" ☐ Yes ☐ No

If Yes - Make a list of the next places you would most like to see in priority sequence.
    If No – go to next category: **"Events"**

B. The next place in the world I would most like to visit is: _____

    1. I would like to go there because: _____

    2. The top 3 things I would like to see there are:

        a. _____

        b. _____

        c. _____

    3. On a scale of 1 -10 (10 being most interesting) I would rank this place # _____

C. The next place in the world I would most like to visit is: _____

    1. I would like to go there because: _____

    2. The top 3 things I would like to see there are:

        a. _____

        b. _____

        c. _____

    3. On a scale of 1 -10 (10 being most interesting) I would rank this place # _____

NOTES

D. The next place in the world I would most like to visit is: _____

   1. I would like to go there because: _____

   2. The top 3 things I would like to see there are:

      a. _____

      b. _____

      c. _____

   3. On a scale of 1 -10 (10 being most interesting) I would rank this place # _____

E. The next place in the world I would most like to visit is: _____

   1. I would like to go there because: _____

   2. The top 3 things I would like to see there are:

      a. _____

      b. _____

      c. _____

   3. On a scale of 1 -10 (10 being most interesting) I would rank this place # _____

NOTES

III. Events:

A. The most exciting event I can imagine attending would be: _____

    1. I would like to attend because: _____

    2. While there, the top 3 things I would like to observe are:

        a. _____

        b. _____

        c. _____

    3. On a scale of 1 -10 (10 being most exciting) I would rank this event # _____

Pose Question: "Is there another exciting event you would love to attend?" ☐ Yes   ☐ No

If Yes - Make a list of the next events you would most like to attend in priority sequence.
    If No – go to next category: **"Activities"**

B. The most exciting event I can imagine attending would be: _____

    1. I would like to attend because: _____

    2. While there, the top 3 things I would like to observe are:

        a. _____

        b. _____

        c. _____

    3. On a scale of 1 -10 (10 being most exciting) I would rank this event # _____

C. The most exciting event I can imagine attending would be: _____

    1. I would like to attend because: _____

    2. While there, the top 3 things I would like to observe are:

        a. _____

        b. _____

        c. _____

    3. On a scale of 1 -10 (10 being most exciting) I would rank this event # _____

NOTES

D. The most exciting event I can imagine attending would be: _____

   1. I would like to attend because: _____

   2. While there, the top 3 things I would like to observe are:

      a. _____

      b. _____

      c. _____

   3. On a scale of 1 -10 (10 being most exciting) I would rank this event # _____

E. The most exciting event I can imagine attending would be: _____

   1. I would like to attend because: _____

   2. While there, the top 3 things I would like to observe are:

      a. _____

      b. _____

      c. _____

   3. On a scale of 1 -10 (10 being most exciting) I would rank this event # _____

NOTES

IV. Activities: (e.g., parachute jumping, extreme skiing, writing a book)

A. The most important thing I would like to do or achieve in my life would be: _____

   1. Accomplishing this would be important because: _____

   2. To accomplish this, I would be willing to do the following things:

      a. _____

      b. _____

      c. _____

   3. On a scale of 1 -10 (10 being most fulfilling) I would rank this activity # _____

Pose Question: "Is there another life-fulfilling activity you would like to do or achieve?" ☐ Yes ☐ No

If Yes - Make a list of the next activities you would most like to do in priority sequence.
If No – go to next category: **"Experiences"**

B. The most important thing I would like to do or achieve in my life would be: _____

   1. Accomplishing this would be important because: _____

   2. To accomplish this, I would be willing to do the following things:

      a. _____

      b. _____

      c. _____

   3. On a scale of 1 -10 (10 being most fulfilling) I would rank this activity # _____

C. The most important thing I would like to do or achieve in my life would be: _____

   1. Accomplishing this would be important because: _____

   2. To accomplish this, I would be willing to do the following things:

      a. _____

      b. _____

      c. _____

   3. On a scale of 1 -10 (10 being most fulfilling) I would rank this activity # _____

NOTES

D. The most important thing I would like to do or achieve in my life would be: _____

    1. Accomplishing this would be important because: _____

    2. To accomplish this, I would be willing to do the following things:

        a. _____

        b. _____

        c. _____

    3. On a scale of 1 -10 (10 being most fulfilling) I would rank this activity # _____

E. The most important thing I would like to do or achieve in my life would be: _____

    1. Accomplishing this would be important because: _____

    2. To accomplish this, I would be willing to do the following things:

        a. _____

        b. _____

        c. _____

    3. On a scale of 1 -10 (10 being most fulfilling) I would rank this activity # _____

Notes

V. Experiences: (e.g., sleeping under the stars of the southern hemisphere)

A. The most thrilling or profound experience I can imagine would be: _____

    1. I would like to experience this because: _____

    2. To experience this, I would be willing to do the following things:

        a. _____

        b. _____

        c. _____

    3. On a scale of 1 -10 (10 being most exciting) I would rank this experience # _____

Pose Question: "Is there another thrilling or profound experience you would like to have?" ☐ Yes   ☐ No

If Yes - Make a list of the next activities you would most like to do in priority sequence.
    If No – go to next category: **"Next Steps"**

B. The most thrilling or profound experience I can imagine would be: _____

    1. I would like to experience this because: _____

    2. To experience this, I would be willing to do the following things:

        a. _____

        b. _____

        c. _____

    3. On a scale of 1 -10 (10 being most exciting) I would rank this experience # _____

C. The most thrilling or profound experience I can imagine would be: _____

    1. I would like to experience this because: _____

    2. To experience this, I would be willing to do the following things:

        a. _____

        b. _____

        c. _____

    3. On a scale of 1 -10 (10 being most exciting) I would rank this experience # _____

NOTES

D. The most thrilling or profound experience I can imagine would be: _____

    1. I would like to experience this because: _____

    2. To experience this, I would be willing to do the following things:

        a. _____

        b. _____

        c. _____

    3. On a scale of 1 -10 (10 being most exciting) I would rank this experience # _____

E. The most thrilling or profound experience I can imagine would be: _____

    1. I would like to experience this because: _____

    2. To experience this, I would be willing to do the following things:

        a. _____

        b. _____

        c. _____

    3. On a scale of 1 -10 (10 being most exciting) I would rank this experience # _____

Notes

VI. Next Steps: You should now have identified approximately 25 items and prioritized them within each of the 5 categories.

A. Create your "Bucket List Summary," which lists all of the items you have entered and reprioritize them in order of importance to you.

B. Review this list and, if necessary, add, delete, edit or change the order of items.

C. You should now have your Bucket List with the top ranked choices in descending order of priority.

D. Review your "Bucket List Summary" and select your "Top 10" most desired items you would like to accomplish. Now reprioritize your "Top 10" items.

E. We now move to the research phase for this "Top 10" List. In the above questionnaire, you provided information on why each of these selections was important to you. You should now determine:

1. When do you see yourself initiating the items?

2. Where will you be traveling to (if it is not in your local area)?

3. With whom will you be doing this?

4. What preparation will be required?

5. How much will it cost?

6. How long will it take (total time away)?

NOTES

Priority List:

1. _____
2. _____
3. _____
4. _____
5. _____
6. _____
7. _____
8. _____
9. _____
10. _____
11. _____
12. _____
13. _____
14. _____
15. _____
16. _____
17. _____
18. _____
19. _____
20. _____
21. _____
22. _____
23. _____
24. _____
25. _____

NOTES

In Summary:

The exercise of creating your Bucket List can be one of the most liberating experiences in life. Many of us have long wanted to meet a special person, visit a particular site, experience something truly amazing, or accomplish something meaningful to us.

The Next Chapter is before you and creating your Bucket List is an invaluable exercise to ensure that you and your partner give voice to your dreams so you can look back on those shared memories and smile forever.

"As empty-nesters, this is the time to rediscover the dreams you put on hold, while you can"

NOTES

8

CHOOSING MY REAL ESTATE DOWNSIZING COACH

Experience has shown that couples who have created a plan before making lifestyle downsizing decisions are more likely to arrive safely at their desired "Next Chapter" destination.

As we have discussed at length in *The Book on Downsizing*, it's crucial that you and your partner first agree on the *"What, When, Why, Who, and How Much"* questions related to your "Next Chapter". Once you have reached consensus on these five questions, answering the *"Where"* question is much easier. Invariably, it's also a more accurate reflection of the "Next Chapter" lifestyle you have defined.

Why do I need a Real Estate & Downsizing Coach?

Simply put, developing a Downsizing Plan incorporates every aspect of your life and is easier to navigate with a "quarterback" who can be an objective resource. Your financial planner, lawyer, realtor, and insurance agent may have your best interests at heart; however, it's important to choose the right resource to help you pull together all of the aspects required for your personalized Downsizing Lifestyle Plan.

> "ENJOY THE JOURNEY, BUT DON'T ALLOW YOURSELF TO MOVE IN EMOTIONALLY UNTIL THE DEAL IS DONE!"

What defines a qualified Real Estate & Downsizing Coach?

It has been our experience that Baby Boomers and Downsizers prefer to work with a professional who has personal experience with the lifestyle challenges they face. When asked what traits were most valuable to them, the most common responses were patience, maturity, and first-hand life experience ("been there and lived through that!").

While there was often a sense of urgency involved in making family, home and lifestyle choices during your child-rearing and career growth years, making midlife decisions seems different. When couples are developing their Downsizing Plan, they take more time for reflection, soul searching and dreaming about the lifestyle they truly want to live in the "Next Chapter". However, they also want a coach who can help them remain objective and realistic in assessing these choices.

> "A QUALIFIED REAL ESTATE & DOWNSIZING COACH CAN HELP TO FACILITATE YOUR DOWNSIZING PLAN AND MAKE IT A REALITY"

NOTES

While your Real Estate & Downsizing Coach is a licensed realtor, he or she can also be said to have "heart," as well as personal midlife experience, business savvy and the patience to allow each client to complete their individual Downsizing assessments. To qualify as a Real Estate & Downsizing Coach, an individual must be a licensed realtor able to trade in your area and have completed the required certification process. If you're interested in finding a certified Real Estate & Downsizing Coach in your area, go to www.TheBookOnDownsizing.com and select "Contact Us".

What Should I Do Before Engaging a Real Estate & Downsizing Coach?

A. The first step is to read *The Book on Downsizing*, a self-paced guide that will assist you in understanding the process of *designing the rest of your life*. Based on more than 10,000 hours of face-to-face conversations with couples who were making the myriad lifestyle decisions associated with rightsizing their life, this first-of-a-kind book incorporates their collective wisdom, experiences, and insights.

B. This workbook has been created to provide you with a step by step guide to discover the "Next Chapter" lifestyle you and your partner truly want, one that matches your personal preparedness.

C. Having completed the workbook questionnaires, your Real Estate & Downsizing Coach can now be of great value. In reviewing the pertinent data from your assessment with you, they can understand your priorities and answer your questions regarding next steps and timing. Being able to discuss your questions and concerns regarding lifestyle choices is easier with the objective advice and experience of a coach to draw on.

D. After discussing "My Downsizing Questions Answered" with your coach, you are ready to review "My Downsizing Home Profile." This will also provide your coach with an overview of the Next Chapter home and neighborhood you and your partner have defined.

How Do I Choose a Real Estate & Downsizing Coach Best Suited to Our Needs?

A. As in any profession, real estate practitioners are required to complete a common curriculum. However, individual skills and personal style may be quite different, so it's crucial to find someone whose personality and approach resonates with you.

B. Prior to interviewing potential coaches who may market their services to a specific segment of the market (e.g., Baby Boomers and Downsizers), you may want to review their resume and their experience dealing with Downsizing and "Next Chapter" planning.

C. Once you've selected a Real Estate & Downsizing Coach you feel is truly committed to your goals and is able to assist you in making the right decisions at each step of the process, you'll be able to move ahead quickly to realize the Downsizing Plan that you and your partner have developed.

D. Should you have questions regarding the process of selecting a realtor, or wish to be connected with a qualified Real Estate & Downsizing Coach in your area, **go to** www.TheBookOnDownsizing.com and select "Contact Us".

NOTES

E. If the information in *The Book on Downsizing* resonated with you and the assessments you have completed in this workbook have been helpful, you're invited to contact the authors by going to www.TheBookOnDownsizing.com and select "Contact Us".

NOTES